B-24 Liberator

Combat Photographs from the European Theater of Operations

BOB LIVINGSTONE

HISTORIC MILITARY AIRCRAFT SERIES, VOLUME 21

Front cover image: A formation of B-24s from 706th Bomb Squadron (BS), 446th Bomb Group (BG), 8th Air Force (AF), on climb from their UK base at Bungay in Suffolk on November 11, 1944, bound for Bottrop in the industrial Ruhr area of Germany. In the foreground is B-24J-155-CO 44-40268, which was later named *Kentucky Belle*, that had previously flown 13 missions with 849th BS, 490th BG, before being transferred to the 446th. It flew a further 69 missions with 706th BS, survived the war, returned to the US, and was last seen parked in the huge salvage yard at Altus, Oklahoma, in October 1945.

Title page image: The majority of these brand-new Ford-built B-24s seen at Willow Run, Michigan, awaiting test flying before being checked and accepted by the United States Army Air Forces (USAAF) Ford representatives would be earmarked for Europe. Air Transport Command (ATC) ferry crews would then fly them to the appropriate center in the US for modifications specific to their intended destinations. Further ferrying would take them to the embarkation airfields and their respective combat theaters, where they would be pooled until needed as a combat unit replacement. It took a lot of organization to build and place a B-24 in combat in World War Two.

Published by Key Books
An imprint of Key Publishing Ltd
PO Box 100
Stamford
Lincs PE9 1XQ

www.keypublishing.com

The right of Bob Livingstone to be identified as the author of this book has been asserted in accordance with the Copyright, Designs and Patents Act 1988 Sections 77 and 78.

Copyright © Bob Livingstone, 2022

ISBN 978 1 80282 457 5

All rights reserved. Reproduction in whole or in part in any form whatsoever or by any means is strictly prohibited without the prior permission of the Publisher.

Typeset by SJmagic DESIGN SERVICES, India.

Introduction

If there is one thing about the B-24 that places it in the historical record above its many competitors, it is its production numbers. Though outclassed by single-engine types, such as the Supermarine Spitfire, Messerschmitt Bf 109, Ilyushin Shturmovik, and, moving closer to the modern era, the Cessna C-172, the Consolidated B-24 Liberator holds the record for the greatest production numbers for any four-engine aircraft, civil or military, ever built.

Like most aircraft of its time, the B-24 traveled a long way from prototype to its final iteration, but its basic airframe remained the same throughout, even in the developed B-24N, which was too late to see production for World War Two. The last of this model culminated in a total of 19,256 B-24 airframes, which included the PB4Y-2 specifically built for the US Navy, which were separate from the PB4Y-1, which came from Army stocks.

The genesis of the B-24 lies in the US Army Air Corps' (USAAC) need to increase production numbers of Boeing's B-17. When approached with a proposal to build the B-17 under license, Consolidated Aircraft Company (CAC) countered with an alternative design of its own, which had a new fuselage but used major design components of its existing flying boat designs for the US Navy to speed lead-time before a first flight.

The design team quickly drew a landplane fuselage with two bomb bays each the same size of the B-17's and an unusual, for the time, a nosewheel undercarriage, to which they attached the tailplane and Davis high aspect-ratio wing from the Model 31 flying boat and four engine nacelles from the PBY.

This bastard son was awarded a Type Certification from the USAAC, which led to an Army contract being signed on March 30, 1939; the CAC Model 32 was born. CAC worked quickly, and the XB-24 made its maiden flight on December 29, 1939. As would be expected, the prototype evolved with various modifications as production of contracted airframes for the AAC began and British and French orders approached.

CAC had previously relocated from the US East Coast to San Diego because of the weather, and much of the early production was carried out in the California sunshine. The first to roll out were the AAC's YB-24s, redirected to the Royal Air Force (RAF) as LB-30As, the first of which flew on January 17, 1941. Twenty Liberator Is followed, then the AAC's sole YB-24 and nine B-24As. The French LB-30s followed, but by this time, France had fallen to the German advance, and these were converted into a Liberator II contract for the RAF. All these aircraft were "embryo B-24s," without self-sealing fuel tanks and engine turbochargers limiting their cruising/bombing altitude, and only the Liberator IIs had the lengthened nose enabling crew access for a navigator and bombardier and deepened rear fuselage capable of accepting a powered tail turret.

The nine B-24Cs can be considered the first "true" B-24s, the first of which was delivered post-Pearl Harbor with turbocharged engines (thus the change from circular engine cowls to the oval) and power turrets in the tail and upper fuselage. Concurrent with the B-24Cs, the first B-24Ds were delivered; the career of the B-24 as a significant weapon of war had begun by January 1942, and it continued until the last ones to be accepted by the US Army Air Forces (AAF) were a Convair (as Consolidated had become by then) B-24M-45-CO on June 5, 1945, and a B-24M-30-FO from Ford (Willow Run) on June 30, 1945.

The other factor that made both the B-24 and the B-17 so significant in the bombing war was the industrial capacity of the US, permitting multi-factory production under license of both types, the B-24 being fabricated by CAC at San Diego, Ford at Willow Run, Michigan, and North American at Dallas, Texas, and assembled at San Diego, CAC Fort Worth, Texas, Dallas, and Douglas at Tulsa, Oklahoma. In the event, Ford (which never ran at full capacity) built almost 7,000 B-24s, a further 1,900 as kits assembled at Tulsa and Fort Worth, and an enormous quantity of spare parts. This capacity meant that, by war's end, B-24s were being produced faster than the AAF could accept them.

The B-24 was not generally as well regarded by aircrews as the B-17, often disparagingly referred to as the "Boxcar" or "the Box the B-17 came in." It burned quickly if a wing tank leaked into the bomb bay, it was definitely not an aircraft to ditch as the bomb bay doors would tear off and the aircraft sank quickly; even a crash landing was dangerous, as the upper turret invariably fell into the cockpit and the fuselage twisted. It was that big bomb bay that weakened the structure.

It was said that a heavily loaded B-24 only became airborne because of the curvature of the earth, and that the wing could not carry enough ice to chill a highball. That wing meant that, at the altitudes required for bombing in Europe, it was hard to hold in steady formation. That and the fact that it was faster than the B-17 meant that the 8th Air Force quickly stopped employing mixed B-17 and B-24 bombing formations. The nosewheel was weak, and heavy landings, side loads, and shimmy caused many a B-24 to imitate a gopher.

The aircraft that started it all – the B-24 prototype, 39-556, on a photographic flight in the San Diego, California, area on February 27, 1940.

It did, however, have redeeming features. Despite its reputation for weakness, it could, and did, absorb surprising amounts of flak or machine gun damage and still make it home. It could carry a big load of bombs, and its range well exceeded that of the B-17, which could be extended even further by filling one of the bomb bays with a fuel bladder. The exceptionally low drag wing, combined with judicious power, boost and fuel mixture settings, enabled airborne times on anti-submarine patrols to exceed 24 hours. The twin-row Pratt & Whitney engines were more reliable than the single-row Curtiss engines of the B-17.

The design lent itself to many roles other than pure bombing. The RAF used its early Liberators as long-range transports (as did the USAAF, particularly with the B-24As), and later models were greatly valued by the RAF and US Navy and Marines as long-range anti-submarine patrol aircraft, enabling the RAF to close the "air-sea gap" over the convoy routes from bases in Iceland.

The long range was particularly significant in the Pacific theater; the Pacific Ocean is huge, with only small islands or island chains hundreds of miles apart. When many of these were occupied by the enemy, the return flight distances were significant, and only the B-24 or a naval fleet could deal with it.

As technology improved, B-24s were flying at night, finding and sinking ships, unseen by their crews. Others were in the forefront of the offense, ranging ahead of missions, again at night, searching for enemy radar stations and plotting their locations for later "killer" B-24s or B-25s to remove the enemy's eyes; others flew long-range weather missions. European Pathfinder operations could be flown by both B-17s and B-24s. It really was a war-winner.

The AAF fielded a number of air forces in various parts of the world as campaigns spread in World War Two, each with their own facilities and groups of aircraft types, depending on the requirements of the region and enemy they fought against. Most had heavy bombers, B-17s or B-24s or both.

The UK-based European Theater 8th Air Force was by far and away the largest operator of the B-24, fielding a total of 15 heavy bomb groups by the end of the war, and it was mainly in the daylight high-altitude bombing role in large formations in combination with its other heavy bomber, the Boeing B-17. Initial missions were flown from mid-August 1942 with B-17s, the first B-24-equipped group, the 93rd, flying its first mission from Alconbury on October 9, 1942, quickly followed by the 44th Bomb Group on November 7, from Shipdham. Many more followed. The photographs that follow try to feature as many of them as possible.

B-24D 41-23819 *Rugged Buggy*, **an original aircraft at the formation of 68th Bomb Squadron (BS), 44th Bomb Group (BG), in September 1942, is shown cruising in a clear late-winter British sky in 1943. This aircraft was shot down on May 14, 1943, by a fighter over Kiel, Germany, after earlier antiaircraft (AA) fire damage. Lost with the aircraft was 68th BS Commanding Officer, Major James E. O'Brien, who survived to become a prisoner of war (POW).**

B-24 Liberator

Combat Photographs from the European Theater of Operations

A very fresh-looking crew of B-24D 41-23682 *The Blasted Event* of 329th BS, 93rd BG, soon after arriving at their English base at Alconbury in early September 1942. In February 1943, this aircraft was "divorced" from the group to take part in Operation *Moling* but had returned in time to take part in the famous August 1, 1943, low-level *Tidal Wave* mission against the Ploești oil refineries. It was later modified for *Carpetbagger* missions and was lost in a nosewheel collapse at Harrington in November 1944 with 492nd BG.

Bomerang, the famously misspelled name of 93rd BG's 328th BS's B-24D 41-23722, was 8th Air Force's (AF) first B-24 to fly 50 missions, twice as many as aircrew were originally expected to fly. It flew missions until August 1943 and returned to the US in mid-April 1944, only to be unceremoniously salvaged on May 30.

The cruelty of war. This wreckage field on Mount Fagradalsfjall, near Grindavik, Iceland, had been 93rd BG's 330th BS's B-24D 41-23728 *Hot Stuff*, the first B-24 in the 8th AF to summit 25 missions (on February 7, 1943) and was matched with a 25-mission crew headed by Captain "Shine" Shannon to return to the US on May 3, 1943. Lieutenant General Frank M. Andrews, Commander of the European Theater of Operations (ETO), summoned to Washington DC, hitched a ride on *Hot Stuff* with his team, forcing five of the crew to remain behind. The weather at their destination, Reykjavik, was snow squalls, low clouds and rain, and while circling to find the airfield they hit near the top of the 1,600ft mountain; only the tail gunner survived.

Johnnie Reb, B-24H 42-50372 of 409th BS, 93rd BG, with another squadron's B-24H formating behind, passes low over a pair of tramp steamers during a practice flight. It joined the 93rd in May 1944, had as uneventful a life as any aircraft in the European war could have, returned to the US in May 1945, and was handed to the Reconstruction Finance Corporation at Altus, Oklahoma, late in October that year for salvage.

Photographed during the night shift at the Willow Run Ford plant is B-24M-10-FO 44-50781, after what appears to have been an unsuccessful test flight: No. 1 engine is missing its propeller and No. 2 prop is feathered. B-24s were difficult to fly with two engines out on one side. While it appears not to have flown in combat, it was delivered to 93rd BG right at the end of the war in late April or early May 1945, at least in time to be named *Little Mike*. It was flown home and stored at Kingman, Arizona, in October 1945 to await its fate.

An unidentified Radio Countermeasures (RCM) crew of 330th BS, 93rd BG, photographed beside B-24J-110-CO 42-109867 *"Maulin' Mallard."* The aircraft bears 8th AF field modifications that were carried out on arrival in the UK at Base Air Depot (BAD) 2, Warton: the armor plate for side protection (both sides) for the pilots and the "K-Bar" navigator's window. 330th BS applied the "Sharkmouth" to the majority of its aircraft (there is another in the background). *"Maulin' Mallard"* flew 115 missions and returned to the US on May 25, 1945, for salvage.

An original cadre aircraft of 328th BS, 93rd BG, B-24D 41-23729 *Shoot Luke*, is shown bombing up with 500-pounders only weeks before its loss in the North Sea on a diversion mission on October 18, 1943. The fuselage star has been greyed out, including the yellow circle that was added to the star during the 328th BS's temporary duty (TDY) with 9th AF for the Ploeşti mission in August. *Shoot Luke* flew on the mission but returned early when its No. 4 engine failed. Note the Dark Olive Drab camouflage "splotched" with Medium Green.

Relatively new B-24J-90-CO 42-100294 *Victory Belle* of 328th BS cruising over Occupied Europe with many other aircraft of 93rd BG. On June 24, 1944, it was shot down at Treon, France, by flak while on a post-D-Day mission against tactical targets.

A "stranger in a strange land." 328th BS, 93rd BG, B-24D 42-40128 named *War Baby* on the right nose and *Ball of Fire the III* on the left was damaged on November 18, 1943, by AA fire while on a mission to Oslo/Kjeller and landed at Bulltofta (Malmö), where it was interned for the duration. It was returned to the UK in September 1945, where it was decided that was not sufficiently airworthy to return to the US and was scrapped.

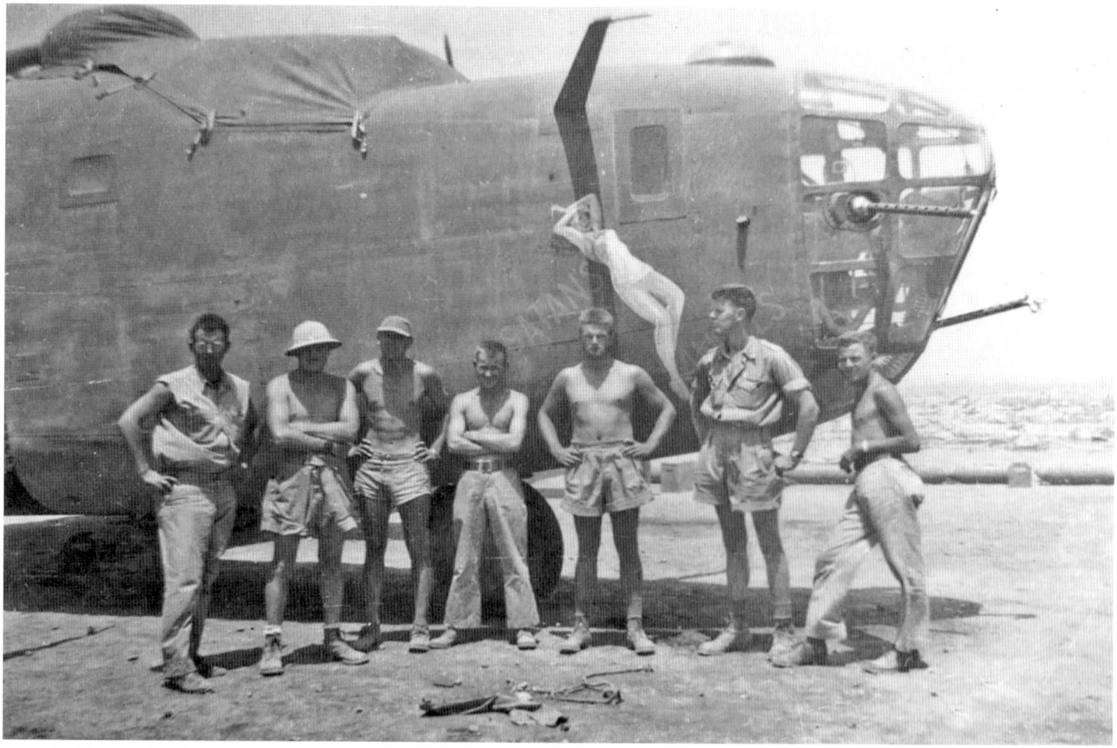

A typically scruffy-looking 328th BS crew beside their 93rd BG B-24D 42-40604 *Satan's Angels* in the North African desert during 9th AF Ploești TDY period. The artwork, with major variations, appeared on both sides of the nose. *Satan's Angels*, piloted by Lts Herrell Ford and Robert McCaffery, flew the mission and bombed, acquiring only a few small holes in the process. On completion of the TDY, the aircraft returned to the UK and was lost on November 13, 1943, after a nosewheel collapse during a crash-landing at Lympne, after which it was reduced to spares.

Lined up behind Anthony Eden (making the broadcast) and Lt General Jacob L. Devers, and in front of B-24D 41-23811 *Fascinatin' Witch* at 44th BG's base at Shipdham, are Captain Bob "Rum Runner" Miller (far left) and other, mainly NCO, crewmen of 66th BS on June 25, 1943. One of the original cadre of 44th BG assigned on September 20, 1942, *Fascinatin' Witch* was shot down by a fighter or fighters during the mission against Wiener Neustadt on October 1, 1943.

Not a B-24 as such, but an early model Liberator known to the AAF as an LB-30 and to the RAF as a Liberator II, AL574 *Commando* was Prime Minister Churchill's personal aircraft used throughout unoccupied Europe and particularly for Atlantic crossings to the US. Originally in full RAF night bomber scheme of Dark Green/Dark Earth uppers and black undersides, here it is stripped of paint. Later still, it returned to CAC for major modifications.

In no doubt a scene staged for the photographer, maintenance personnel of 44th BG on work stands investigate the No. 1 engine of a B-24D in early April 1943. The problem appears real enough as the propeller is feathered, and the prop dome is set to be removed. Despite the date, it must still be cold, as all are wearing leather flying jackets, which was not normal wear for a maintenance crew.

On a winter day at Shipdham in 1943, 44th BG ground crew gather around the Church Army mobile canteen for a hot drink and a snack while 68th BS B-24D 41-23816 *Black Jack* looms behind. The Church of England provided services like this in both world wars. This B-24, so named because the digits 123816 add up to 21, was lost over Wiener Neustadt on October 1, 1943, while on TDY with 9th AF, breaking up in the air after a direct AA hit.

The backbone of 8th AF, a B-24H, in this case 42-95049 *Fearless Fosdick, Writ by Hand*, warms its engines on its 67th BS hardstand. This Ford-built and assembled H-25 is the almost fully developed B-24 with the electric Emerson nose turret, enlarged "chin" piece for the bombardier and carrying 8th AF field modifications of armor plates on the cockpit sides and pilot's windshield and navigator's bubble window. It was delivered to 44th BG in spring 1944 and was abandoned by its crew on March 1, 1945, over San Quentin, France, after running out of fuel caused by battle damage.

Originally named *Minerva* as one of the original cadre of 93rd BG, B-24D 41-23689 was transferred as "war weary" (non-combat-worthy) for use as an assembly ship for 329th BS in January 1944. This paint job was based on an experimental camouflage on another aircraft in the US. Originally retaining, and usually photographed with, its turrets and guns, it is seen here in its lightened form in summer 1944. On November 13, 1944, it suffered a take-off accident and was written off.

A rare image from the Douglas Archives shows two early production B-24Hs from the Tulsa factory in September 1943. 41-28591 on the left, the 18th off the line, became *Inspector's Squawks* of 753rd BS, 453rd BG, and was shot down in the target area on a Berlin mission on June 21, 1944. All crew became POWs. The other, 41-28594, became *Supermouse* of 719th BS, 449th BG (15th AF), and on January 15, 1944, after two engines on one side lost power off the coast of Italy, four crew bailed out and were rescued, while the remainder were killed in an attempted ditching.

Originally captioned as the first Pathfinder (PFF) aircraft (41-28653) and crew from 482nd BG to fly to Berlin (on March 6, 1944), records show that Capt Larson (far right rear) flew as Deputy Lead in 389th BG PFF aircraft 41-28696 on that day. Actor Jimmy Stewart actually flew as air commander on '653 for 445th BG on March 18. After May 29, 1945, the serial disappears from combat records, and it probably remained at Alconbury with the 482nd as a PFF crew trainer. The write-off date in May 1945 is considered to be a "paper" date, as it almost certainly was salvaged somewhat earlier.

Boresighting the nose turret guns on B-24H 41-28735 at Tulsa in October 1944. On arrival in the ETO after 8th AF theater modifications, '735 was assigned to 458th BG, but after seven months of operations, the aircraft crash-landed at Shipdham on a *Truckin'* mission to Lille on September 21, 1944; its right main landing gear was broken off and the fuselage badly damaged, and it was declared Category 5 damage and written off.

In total, 120 8th AF Douglas (Tulsa) B-24Hs were modified for 8th AF as Pathfinders (i.e., with H2X radar equipment) to improve bombing accuracy and in an attempt to reduce mission weather cancellations by telling the group when to bomb. The original idea was to have an all-Pathfinder group, the 482nd, which could assign individual aircraft to lead other groups on missions. One such was 41-28785, shown on September 21, 1944, already under salvage after crash-landing on the Continent while on loan to the 458th BG for post-D-Day *Truckin'* missions. Later, the idea of a specific PFF Group was abandoned, and PFF aircraft flown by trained crews were assigned to each group.

A good example of 8th AF combat conditions: a small part of a 446th BG incursion into Germany in the face of moderate flak in early April 1945. Remember that each of those innocent-looking black puffs contains many small slivers of steel, any one of which could take the life of an individual crewman or damage a vital component and decide the fate of an entire crew. The three closest aircraft are all B-24Hs of 705th BS (left to right): 42-94941 *Pin Up Girl*, 42-50629 and 41-28814. Of these three, only 42-50629 survived the war and returned to the US.

Sitting on the Douglas, Tulsa, hardstand before delivery to the USAAF is B-24H-15-DT 41-28883. On arrival in the ETO, it was assigned to 762nd BS, 460th BG. On May 10, 1944, it received a direct AA hit over Wiener Neustadt, which started a cockpit fire. Six crew members bailed out, but the fire was controlled, and the aircraft returned to base. After repair, it was lost over Graz, Austria, on October 16, 1944. The crew bailed out on the northern side of the town and landed in Yugoslavia.

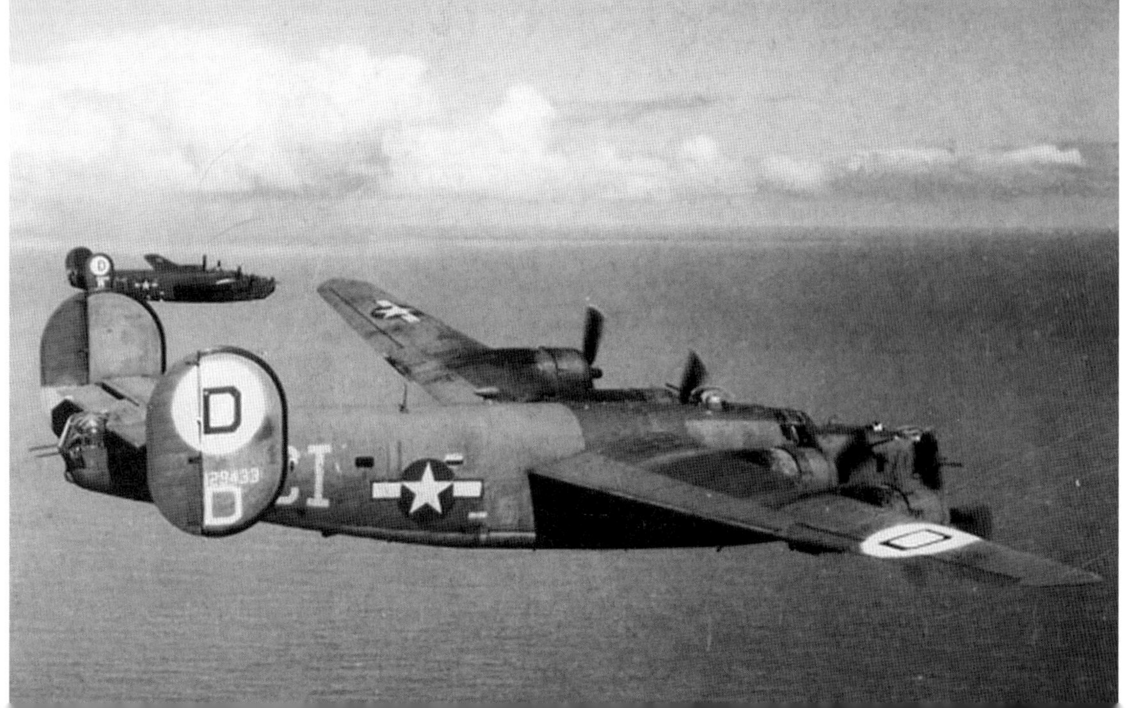

B-24H 41-28948 of 565th BS, 389th BG, was damaged by flak on the Munich mission of July 12, 1944, and force-landed at Basle-Birsfelden, Basel-Landschaft, Switzerland. The photo shows the aircraft post-war (note no guns and no upper turret) after repair at Dubendorf before being ferried back to BAD 1, Burtonwood, Lancashire, on October 15, 1945, where it was salvaged.

B-24H 41-29433 – known to its crew as *Sons of America* but not painted on – of 576th BS, 392nd BG, during a test flight prior to the group's Mission 95 to Politz on May 29, 1944. The group lost six aircraft on this mission, mainly to the estimated 75–100 single- and twin-engine fighters encountered over the target. Of eight badly damaged aircraft, two were abandoned by their crews after reaching England. Lt A. W. Evans' crew bailed out of '433 west of their Wendling base and all landed safely.

B-24H 41-29542, original equipment of 18th BS, 34th BG, is seen high over England in June 1944, before the application of the new 8th AF hi-vis markings. The 34th re-equipped with the B-17 in July–August 1944 and '542 was transferred to 445th BG as a replacement for 702nd BS. On the September 27, 1944, Kassel mission, '542 was badly mauled by fighters that killed the upper turret and tail gunners. The rest of the crew bailed out; the copilot being beaten to death by German civilians and the remaining seven becoming POWs.

A view of the modification line of the Consolidated Fort Worth facility in late May 1943. On the left are B-24Ds, which were built at San Diego and are being converted for the anti-submarine (AS) role, and on the right are C-87 conversions. Front and center is 42-40823 in its White under Olive Drab uppers, which was further converted at Olmstead with the "Droop Snoot" modification that added a nose turret. In the ETO, it operated with 19th AS Squadron, 479th AS Group, from St Eval and Dunkeswell until October 1943, when the US Navy took over AS operations with PB4Y-1s. 42-40823 became a CB-24 (transport) with 2nd Bomb Division in the UK until it was salvaged as war weary in November 1944.

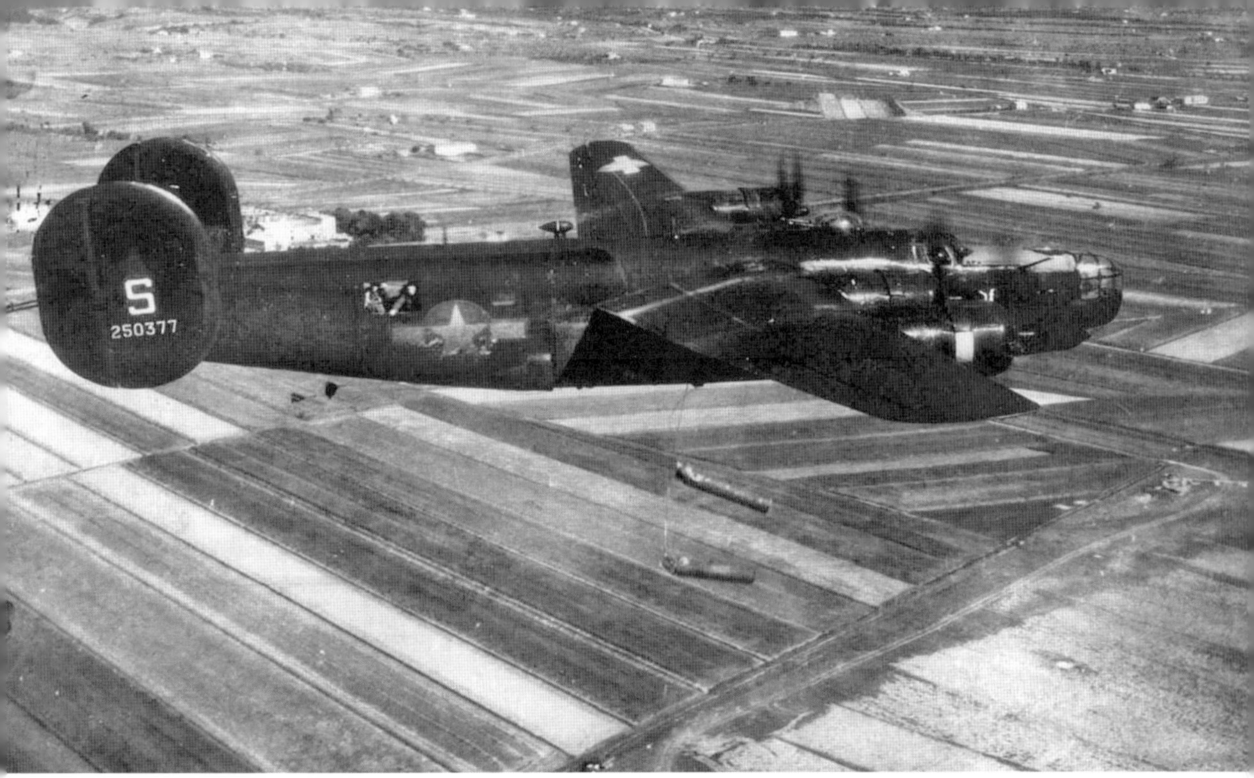

B-24H 42-50377 was converted for the *Carpetbagger* role and painted black for night operations at low level over Occupied Europe – note the modified nose without turret. It operated initially with 859th BS, 801st BG (Provisional), until the role was given greater resources when 492nd BG was re-organized from a Bomb Group to a *Carpetbagger* Group. 42-50377 is shown here in Italy on a practice Storepedo drop after the *Carpetbagger* role diminished after D-Day and 859th BS was transferred to 15th Special Operations Group (Provisional), 15th AF, in December 1944.

An indication of the massive production capacity of the Ford B-24 factory at Willow Run, Ypsilanti, Michigan, on September 11, 1944, with completed cockpit and rear fuselages in store waiting for movement to the assembly area or to be packed to be sent to the other factories that assembled B-24s built by Ford. Nose turrets had their own prefabricated modules ready to be attached to the cockpit sections and the wings lie out of sight nearby.

An unusual photograph of a distressing incident. On April 14, 1945, during the bomb run mission to tactical targets on the banks of the River Gironde estuary, a B-17 group and a B-24 group ended up over the same space when the higher B-17s dropped their fragmentation bombs. Five B-24s of 567th BS, 389th BG, were hit, with three damaged and two destroyed, as seen in the photo. Eleven airmen were killed. 42-50532, on the left, escaped to a forced landing, while 42-50774 lies inverted in the shallows, having lost its rear fuselage.

Coastal Command Liberator GR.V BZ717 of 59 Squadron RAF. The GR (General Reconnaissance – i.e., Oceanic Patrol and AS) model is basically the GR.III with ASV Mark III centimetric radar (US SCR 517C) installed in the housing in the nose. Later models had SCR717 centimetric radar housed in a retractable dome in place of the belly turret. 59 (GR) Squadron operated from a range of different UK airfields with access to Atlantic patrol areas.

Lovely Lady's Avenger (44-40093 of 786th BS, 466th BG) lies with its back broken short of the runway at Bulltofta, Sweden. Hit in two engines by flak over Berlin on June 21, 1944, it could not maintain height, and with a gunner's parachute shredded by the flak, a bail out was not possible, so they turned for Sweden. Good decision, because they were home in the US and out of the war by Christmas 1944!

B-24J 42-50716 is shown in the US, freshly returned from an apparently uneventful combat career with 706th BS, 446th BG. A rarely noted item, the command deck escape hatch, which was added to ETO aircraft as a theater modification until it entered the production line, can be seen just forward of and below the Automatic Direction Finder (ADF) "football" on the rear fuselage.

Two B-24s of 755th BS, 491st BG, formate briefly over the target. In the foreground is B-24J 42-50757, which has just released its bombs, and the other is one of only eight North American B-24Js to come to 8th AF, 42-78482. Both returned to the US after the war, but '757 had a bumpy ride, having crash-landed near Florrenes, Belgium, after flak damage over Cologne and, in a later accident, collapsed the nosewheel landing at Charleroi.

A fairly well-known crash, but the image is usually presented from the other side; this shot demonstrates that not all B-24 nosewheel collapses were relatively benign. B-24H 42-51112 from 733rd BS, 453rd BG, had just bombed Brunswick on March 31, 1945, when an Me 262 attacked, taking out one engine and badly wounding the navigator. The aircraft made a crash-landing 45km southwest of Hanover with the pictured result. The navigator either died or was killed in the crash, as was the top turret gunner/engineer, and the remaining eight crew members became POWs.

This Douglas-assembled (from Ford parts) B-24H is seen on a pre-delivery test flight from Tulsa; the Ford line number is still visible on the nose. In the ETO, it would have had the theater modifications and then been assigned to 700th BS, 445th BG. It is probably a good thing that the 700th aircrews were not aware that it was late arriving in the UK because it suffered a structural failure on arrival at Goose Bay on the ferry flight from the US. It flew from Christmas Day 1944 through to March 23, 1945, when it was shot down over Munster.

Showing some of the versatility of the B-24 is this 9th Air Force C-109, a conversion of a Ford B-24J-15 into a fuel carrier within tanks in the bomb bay. 42-52033 operated with the IXth Troop Carrier Command, flying fuel into forward areas of Europe to keep the Army's machines running. Its history is undocumented, and even its final fate is unknown, with the AAF not writing it off the books until 1946.

The markings on this B-24H (42-52572) are somewhat deceptive. Originally assigned to 486th BG, the fuselage codes indicate it is assigned to 833rd BS; however, the large "S" in a square on the wing is a 34th BG insignia, as is the tail marking. In June 1944, 486th BG GH navigation-equipped lead aircraft were transferred to the 34th to do the same job, and this was one of them. From September the 34th was flying B-17s, so its tenure was short. What it was doing until it was recorded as salvaged war weary in May 1945 remains a mystery.

42-63775 began its combat life as a 479th AS Group sub-hunter, but when the US Navy wrested that role from the AAF in October 1943, it was released from AS Command and was accepted by VIII Bomber Command, which decided that it would be best utilized for *Carpetbagger* duties. In early December that year, it was undergoing these mods at BAD 1. It progressed through the maze of *Carpetbagger* administrative units until August 1944, when it was locked into 856th BS, 492nd BG. It survived the rigors of low-level night penetration of Occupied Europe until it returned to the US in July 1945, only to be unceremoniously sent to Albuquerque, New Mexico, for salvage.

Known as *Striped Ape II*, but not painted on, this aircraft started out as B-24H 41-29489 *2nd Avenue El* with 486th BG but flew no missions before being transferred to 458th BG and later to the 492nd and, finally in September, after being declared war weary, to the 448th as the group's second assembly ship in maroon, white and black stripes. When it was salvaged by 3 Strategic Air Depot (SAD) at Warton on May 26–31, 1945, the right auxiliary spars were found to be buckled.

B-24H 42-64435 – a B-24 from Consolidated, Fort Worth, with a sad history. The photo shows a brand-new aircraft up for a pre-delivery photo session over southern California in August 1943. It subsequently joined 445th BG, as part of its work-up as a new bomb group in the US. It flew across the Atlantic to the UK in December 1943, as part of the group's original cadre. After theater mods, it was immediately transferred to 392nd BG, which assigned it to 576th BS as a replacement. On February 21, 1944, as the group crossed the English Channel on return from group Mission 39, it was seen with an engine on fire; it never made it home to Wendling and is assumed to have crashed or ditched in the Channel.

This B-24H-20-FO, 42-94947, is an unusual bird in 8th AF, in that all H-20-FOs came from the factory in standard Olive Drab/Dark Grey camouflage but this aircraft is stripped back to natural metal, one of only seven so known in the 8th. Originally named *The Betty-Jim* and in standard paint, it operated with 489th BG, transferring to 854th BS, 491st BG, in late November 1944, photographed here in March 1945. It returned to the US on June 19, 1945, and was placed in storage pending salvage at Altus, Oklahoma, in September.

Like so many combat aircraft, 42-95130 *Spirit of Pocahontas*'s combat career was short, only flying missions with 700th BS, 445th BG, from May 13 to June 21, 1944, when it was forced to ditch after a flak round went through a fuel tank without exploding. Despite the story that a loaded B-24 could only become airborne due to the curvature of the earth, here it is shown rotating on take-off at its home base Tibenham, Norfolk.

The old and the new. A Swedish soldier in a shady spot watches the farmer and his hay rake as they pass some of the 8th AF bombers interned at Bulltofta, Sweden. Both visible aircraft arrived on June 20, 1944, though 42-95135 from 579th BS, 392nd BG, was thought to have been deliberately diverted to Sweden by its crew to avoid further combat. 42-51213 (on the right) was from 704th BS, 446th BG. Both were flown back to the UK in June 1945.

A pleasing photo of B-24H 42-95273 from 709th BS, 467th BG, at the point of bomb release over the target, though I detect the censor's hand on the fins of the Olive Drab aircraft above in painting out the group markings. It appears that the paleness of the same markings on '273 would be enough to hide them if the image was used in a newspaper. 42-95273 was written off in a ground collision with 44-40465 on December 4, 1944.

Pictured at Horsham St. Faith is a line of 458th BG B-24s on the taxiway just short of the runway. Most are shut down, waiting, but the lead aircraft, 42-100408 of 753rd BS, has engines still running, possibly for magneto checks prior to entering the runway for take-off. Originally named *Lady Luck*, the name was lost when the "Beastface" artwork was applied, becoming simply known as *The Beast*. It survived the war and returned to the US for salvage.

Total destruction. New B-24J 42-100409 departed the US for the UK on January 21, 1944, assigned to ATC and bringing a fresh crew as replacements to 8th AF. A few days after arrival, on February 2, 1944, it was being ferried to the modification center for 8th AF, but the British winter weather was poor and the aircraft hit a hill at Barnstaple, North Devon, and all the ferry crew were killed. It was never assigned to a bomb group.

Curious German civilians inspect B-24J 42-110027 of 576th BS, 392nd BG, which crash landed on its 30th mission with a 577th BS crew on June 21, 1944. The bombardier/navigator was found unconscious from an oxygen problem, so the pilot aborted and dropped to 12,000ft, where they were attacked by two Bf 109s. Dropping to tree-top level, they hit at least one tree, were shot at while overflying an airfield, and finally hit the chimney of a house, which caused one engine to catch alight. At this point, the pilot found a field at Aldrup, put the gear down and landed, where the crew were quickly surrounded by soldiers and became POWs.

Looking brand new, 25-mission B-24J 44-40357 of 863rd BS, 493rd BG, climbs slowly past the photographer in early autumn 1944. Not long after this photo was taken, the 493rd converted to the B-17, and the aircraft was transferred to 466th BG, with which it was lost on March 12, 1945, during a mission to the rail marshalling yards at Friedland. It lost two engines, and when a third began to give trouble the crew bailed out. The aircraft entered a flat spin and crashed at Sibbe in the Netherlands.

The full complement of the 96th Troop Carrier Squadron C-109s. The 96th was a squadron of 440th Troop Carrier Group, mainly composed of C-47s. The C-109s were fuel carriers to the post D-Day armies on the Continent. The nearest aircraft, 44-49258, was a conversion of a B-24L-CO and was written off due to enemy action (either fighter strafing or, more likely, artillery fire) on March 25, 1945.

This Pathfinder lead B-24, 44-49610, designated as a B-24L with Gee-H and H2X, is seen after its one and only mission with 791st BS, 467th BG, after collapsing the nosewheel and running off the runway to the side at Rackheath on March 24, 1945. The B-24LSH had the lightweight (handheld machine gun) turret that enabled the copilot to monitor the formation from the turret, while the air commander occupied the copilot's position on the flight deck. There must be unseen damage, because the aircraft was salvaged the next day.

A formation of B-24Ds from 389th BG heads out over a particularly attractive cloudscape. The date is not known, but the tail markings were only introduced in August 1943, so it can safely be assumed that this would have been during the winter of 1943/44, as by spring 1944, the large fuselage codes began to appear. None of the aircraft can be specifically identified.

An unidentified 852nd BS, 491st BG, B-24 crew has just landed back at Metfield after a foray to support the armies fighting on the Continent at a fairly primitive airfield "somewhere in France," as is evidenced by the mud splashed back on the rear fuselage, a common feature of operations on a Marsden Mat runway. The reason for the white in the fuselage insignia being painted out is unknown, as this practice died out in 1943. It was introduced because it was considered (on an Olive Drab painted aircraft) to act as an aiming point for a fighter. It seems to have been common in the 491st, as even their formation monitor, which was unlikely to ever be in combat, also has the same modification.

No, it is not a small B-24; this is the 854th BS, 491st BG, formation monitor, a P-47D-6-RE serialled 42-74670. When preparing for a mission, the bombers would circle in the vicinity of the airfield as the aircraft took off and joined up in their allocated positions. The squadron commander would sometimes join up in this aircraft if there were reports of poor formation holding and verbally chivvy the recalcitrant pilots. It could also be used as a squadron headquarters hack. Note the non-standard Malcolm hood, which is more commonly seen on P-51Cs, and "greyed out" national markings.

This B-24H, 42-52509 *Ain't Miss Behavin'*, is attracting so much attention because it is the first aircraft of 466th BG to land and taxi in from the group's first mission at home base RAF Attlebridge on March 22, 1944. It was operating at this time with 784th BS, but later was transferred to 786th BS. It disappears from 466th BG records after September 11, 1944, and remains untraced until it is recorded as war weary and salvaged on May 29 ,1945.

No pressurized refueling from the wing underside back in 1944. Here, 42-94965 *Angel* of 409th BS, 93rd BG, is taking aboard a calculated load of fuel in the two inboard tanks simultaneously from the standard USAAF "gasoline" tanker at Hardwick prior to a mission. This B-24H crash landed at Villers-la-Chevre, 5km (3 miles) west of Longwy, France, on December 11, 1944, and the last of its wreckage was only finally cleared away in 1948!

One of the most striking nose arts of the ETO is actually the artist's second attempt at this Zodiac portrayal. The first, painted as a one-off, and quite a different interpretation, was lost to 486th BG before the group even began its entry to combat as that aircraft went for theater modification and never returned. This second attempt triggered a series of Zodiac artworks within 834th BS – *Sagittarius*, *Libra*, etc. This photograph shows *Aries* after it had passed to 492nd BG in the *Carpetbagger* role (note the black background). The airframe to which it was applied was B-24H 42-52693, and it survived to be broken up at Altus, Oklahoma, postwar. The artist was Phil Brinkman.

The Air Traffic Control van at Metfield. The controller's "cupola" appears to be the nose piece from a B-17. The day's duty pilot won that job back in World War Two. I'll bet it got hot in there on a warm summer day! This writer spent many years in airconditioned control towers.

Nose art of *Axis Exlax* on B-24H 42-94870 of 848th BS, 490th BG, looking as if it is freshly painted and still in the US. This aircraft, part of the group movement to the UK, appears to have struck some difficulty on the trip, having departed the US on April 28, 1944, but not arriving until June 20. It flew 14 missions with the 490th before being transferred to 702nd BS, 445th BG. It was lost on April 7, 1945, when it was shot down by a fighter and crashed at Bassum.

The quality of the nose art on a bomber was of very uneven quality. Often it was applied in the US by the ferry crew who thought it would be the aircraft they would go to war in, only to find that they and the aircraft would almost always go to different groups. The crews would club together and pay an artist, or a crew member with talent might do it. A good artist at an embarkation airfield could make good money in a side hustle painting nose art. *Back to the Sack*, 44-40249, flew with 854th BS, 491st BG, and returned to the US after the war for salvage at Altus.

The USAAF maintained three major air depots in the UK: Base Air Depots 1, 2 and 3. BAD 1 was at Burtonwood, BAD 2 at Warton (known as "The World's Greatest Air Depot") and BAD 3 at Langford Lodge, Northern Ireland. This is an aerial view of BAD 2 and numerous B-24s can be seen amongst the buildings, which would also be full of B-24s. All three dealt with all types and were responsible for heavy engineering, major overhauls, battle damage repair and design and manufacture of modifications required by 8th AF. Over 10,000 aircraft were processed at BAD 2, including almost 3,000 B-24s.

On November 18, 1943, 2nd Air Division, 8th AF, mounted a bombing mission to Kjeller airfield in Norway. One hundred and seven aircraft from 44th, 93rd, 389th and 392nd bomb groups took off, and while not all made it to the target, it was still a large raid. One B-24 from 578th BS, 392nd BG, was observed at 1145hrs heading towards the Swedish border with one engine smoking heavily. It was B-24H 42-7502 *Bakadori*, and it landed safely at Orebro to be interned for the duration, as seen here.

B-24s of 453rd BG, positioned on the taxiway for take-off, wait for the visual lead aircraft, 42-50317 *Balls O'Fire*, to commence rolling on the runway. Since it is displaying code E- on the tail, the date is prior to May 27, 1944, as on that date it changed to E+. This aircraft flew as many as 60 missions, the last on April 11, 1945. By August 1945, it was to be found at Altus, under the control of the Reconstruction Finance Corporation awaiting salvage.

Bambi, B-24H 41-29567, assembled at Consolidated's Fort Worth factory from Ford parts, began its combat career with 4th BS, 34th BG, and carried the artwork and name on both sides – this configuration not unique but uncommon. When the 34th began re-equipping with the B-17 in October 1944, *Bambi* was transferred to 458th BG and assigned to 752nd BS. The left side artwork was overpainted and new *My Bunnie* artwork added. On December 31, 1944, it force-landed on the Continent but was repaired and returned to the unit on March 2, 1945. It met its final fate at Altus. *My Bunnie* can be seen on p.60.

Betta Duck, 44-40454, was in the early production blocks of the B-24J from Consolidated, incorporating a nose turret and no paint – the best-looking B-24 in my opinion. It began combat in 493rd BG, which was the last BG to join 8th AF and whose first mission was on D-Day, but the B-24 was quickly transferred to 34th BG that month. The photo shows it in 7th BS of that unit, but the 34th transitioned to the B-17 in October, so *Betta Duck* was transferred yet again, this time to 466th BG. Like so many other 8th AF aircraft, it finished at Altus postwar.

Better known as *Hookem Cow* (painted on the left side), *Betty*, B-24H 42-95120 of 755th BS, 458th BG, had a taxi accident at Horsham St. Faith on May 27, 1944, which left it looking like this. Repaired, it flew on until April 14, 1945, when, not long after taking off from the same location in poor weather, the No. 2 engine caught fire, and the aircraft crashed and burned at Hainford near Norwich, killing the crew.

Big Dealer, B-24H 42-94851, carried colorful red and yellow artwork applied by its 7th BS, 34th BG, crew, but they never flew it in combat as it transferred before then to 860th BS, 493rd BG, on May 25, 1944. It suffered a number of mission aborts, so it appears not to have been a particularly reliable mount. It left the 493rd in September as it was re-equipping with B-17s and was converted for *Carpetbagger* missions, joining 406th BS (Night Leaflet) with a shiny black all over paint job, and picked up the name *Mickey Mouse*. It expired at Altus, Oklahoma.

B-24H 42-50387 of 576th BS, 392nd BG, received an unusual honor on August 8, 1944. The American Red Cross (ARC) ran a particularly popular canteen on the 392nd's base at Wendling, and Base Commanding Officer Lt Col Lorin Johnson arranged for a 392nd B-24 be named in honor of the ARC, and Birdie Schmidt was painted on the aircraft by Sergeant Arthur H. Olsen, 578th Engineering Section, and the name *Birdie Schmidt ARC* was added. The next day, the crew in the photograph, all wearing new flying jackets with the aircraft's name on the back, flew a mission in the aircraft, and the left waist gunner, S/Sgt John Komacho (kneeling, second from the right), was badly wounded. The aircraft was finally lost due to mechanical failure over the Continent on February 15, 1945, during a mission to Magdeburg and the crew were taken as POWs.

453rd BG's bomb dump at Old Buckenham. The bombs in the foreground are 500lb, and the one being guided to the pile is 250lb – all high explosives. The lugs that the crane is hooked to connect to the bomb rack in the aircraft. Obviously, none are fused. The tails are only light weight sheet metal and are attached before loading on an aircraft. Fuses are then put in the bombs by the armorers and safetied with a pin that the bombardier will take out when closer to the target. Generally, bombs are relatively safe in this condition, but mistakes or simple stupidity can set one – or all – off. Both the RAF and the USAAF had bomb dumps at airfields explode.

An armorer adjusts the positioning of two 500lb bombs on the bomb trolley beside the aircraft. After fitting the tail to the bombs, the trolley would then be wheeled under the bomb bay and the bombs would be lifted one at a time to the aircraft's bomb rack by winching each up with a wire until the lugs could be hooked to the rack. When all bombs were loaded, the armorer would then fit and safety the fuses.

B-24H 41-29459 *Bonnie* flew only five missions with 784th BS, 466th BG, before being transferred to 700th BS, 445th BG, with which it first flew on June 17, 1944. It was removed from combat before the end of July, and the serial appears in a list of aircraft "being approved to be designated perm unfit for tactical use," dated July 25, 1944. Subsequently, '959 was declared war weary on August 7, 1944, with only 201 hours total time. There must have been something seriously wrong with this aircraft. Although it was to be ferried back to the US immediately, it sat at BAD 3, Langford Lodge, and did not return to the US until September 6, 1945.

This wreck was original 453rd BG equipment flown to the UK in December 1943 named *Cee Gee* and serialled 41-28641. Although a 735th BS aircraft, it was flown before the group entered combat by a newly arrived 732nd BS crew on a training flight on February 3, 1944, during which they became lost and force landed out of fuel and damaged by a fighter at a Luftwaffe airfield in France, thus delivering a complete B-24 to the Germans. Repaired, it flew with KG.200. It was recaptured as seen at Salzburg in May 1945.

Wrong place, wrong time. 42-51184 *Cherry* of 705th BS, 446th BG, had force landed at B-58 (Brussels-Melsbroek) with an engine out during the mission to Bingen on December 10, 1944. The weather was atrocious, and the tactical USAAF was basically grounded for the rest of the year. The Luftwaffe Operation *Bodenplatte* was intended to cripple Allied air forces during the stagnant stage of the Battle of the Bulge so that the German Army could resume its advance. The weather cleared sufficiently on January 1, 1945, and a force of Fw 190s and Me 109s swept across the Low Countries strafing and destroying many Allied aircraft. *Cherry* was just one of them.

Two for the price of one: a pair of 706th BS, 446th BG, B-24Hs cruise over a solid undercast on November 9, 1944. The nearer aircraft, *Dear Marrion*, 42-51272, which arrived in the UK from the US on July 21, 1944, would be lost to AA over Neukirchen in another three weeks exactly. The other, *Home Breaker*, 42-52612, which arrived in March 1944, would go on to survive the war and return to the US and take up residence at Albuquerque Army Air Base (AAB), on July 31, 1945.

67th BS, 44th BG, B-24H 42-51309 attempted a take-off at Shipdham on December 18, 1944, but pilot Lt Collins was unable to prevent the aircraft from sliding off the runway in the prevailing severe icing conditions. The left main undercarriage, unable to take the strain of the side loads, collapsed, and the aircraft spun around in the muddy grass. The winter of 1944/45 was one of the worst in many years.

This all-black B-24H came to 406th Squadron (Night Leaflet) as a new aircraft rather than secondhand from a bomb group, as was the usual case. Unusually, it has retained its nose turret instead of having it removed and replaced with an observer/navigator's position. This aircraft survived the war and was salvaged at Walnut Ridge, Arkansas.

44-50726 is a late war Ford-built B-24M – note the "bay window" style of the navigator's position in the nose – which was assigned to 8th AF headquarters. The war with Germany was officially over on May 7, 1945, and the Danes began planning an air pageant at Copenhagen's Kastrup airfield shortly afterward. The RAF and USAAF were to attend, and this aircraft (note that it is still armed) came to Kastrup as part of the planning. The pageant was delayed, but it finally took place on July 1, 1945. The aircraft was sent to Walnut Ridge for salvage on January 9, 1946.

Aircrew from 506th BS inspect B-24H 42-51704 at Shipdham, looking at the flak damage from a close German 88mm AA round on January 17, 1945. The aircraft was part of a mission to the synthetic oil plant at Ruhland, which was diverted to marshalling yards in Dresden because of weather. 44th BG headquarters feared a disaster had occurred when only 15 of the 33 B-24s dispatched returned to Shipdham, but all but one had landed at other airfields in France or Britain. 42-51704 was quickly repaired but transferred to 68th BS. It survived the war and became one of the many hundreds of AAF aircraft stored at Kingman, Arizona.

Parked on the grass at Dubendorf in Switzerland is 42-100330 from 67th BS, 44th BG, after landing there on April 13, 1944. On the way to bomb Lechfeld, all four engines overheated. Once the bombs had been dropped, full rich fuel mixture and fully open cowl gills made no difference, and, unable to make it back to England, Lt Griffiths headed for Switzerland. The No. 2 engine had to be shut down (the feathered prop can be seen in the photo), and the Swiss fired at them, but they scraped in to be interned.

42-100367 of 67th BS, 44th BG, lies crash-landed short of the runway at Shipdham on July 6, 1944. The report indicates that it lost an engine after take-off on the Kiel mission and returned to land, but the aircraft, fully bombed-up, "faltered" on final and crashed short of the runway. I do note that none of the propellers are feathered, which may have had some bearing on the ability of the aircraft to fly on three engines. Kiel would have been its 37th mission.

44th BG had a bad day on April 8, 1944, when leading the formation, losing eleven aircraft; 42-109827 from 67th BS was one of them. Shot up by fighters at the Initial Point (IP), the aircraft caught fire and four crew managed to bail out before the aircraft exploded, blowing the pilot out of the aircraft. One of the men who bailed out died, so there were six casualties altogether. In this photo, a group of German civilians inspect the shattered tail of the B-24 lying in the country lane beside a house.

Armorers at Mendlesham take a breather on a bomb trolley, waiting for their aircraft to be towed to the hardstand so that they can begin to load these bombs in it. The tails have been attached, this usually only occurring when bombs were to be loaded. Fusing would take place once loading was complete. The aircraft behind them can be identified as from 34th BG by its distinctive half red tail.

Lt Harold Boehm's crew, assigned to one of the "secret squadrons," stand in front of Jackal-equipped B-24H 42-50385 *Beast of Bourbon*, one of the most colorful of the 8th AF Liberators. This aircraft from 36th Squadron (RCM) flew in the Battle of the Bulge jamming German tank communications but crashed on take-off just half a mile west of Cheddington on February 19, 1945.

Big Chief Lil' Beaver, B-24J 42-51514, arrived in the UK on August 13, 1944, and was assigned to 458th BG, which slotted it into 756th BS. It flew missions right up until April 25, 1945, with no apparent drama, accident or damage – a model of a B-24, and one guesses it was not built on a Monday, though of course manufacture of aircraft was a 24/7 affair during the war. It returned to the US postwar and arrived at Altus for storage on November 25, 1945.

After arrival in the UK on July 12, 1944, B-24J 42-95592 was modified at BAD 2, Warton, to become a B-24JSH – a Pathfinder – and assigned to 784th BS, 466th BG, where it gained its *Black Cat* name and artwork. Almost hidden by the propeller shadow is the exhaust outlet for the electronics that confirms its Pathfinder status, and it would also have carried an H2X radar in place of the ball turret. It so nearly survived the war, being shot down on April 21, 1945, by flak over Regensburg.

The Briggs-Sperry Model 13 ventral ball turret fitted to most B-24s (not the early B-24Ds or the H2X radar Pathfinders). Because of the low fuselage clearance of the B-24, it had to be retractable, suspended from a heavy roof support by a hydraulic retraction ram that rotated through 360°. It was entered in the fuselage by the gunner, and the entry hatch became his back rest. The ball gunner was usually the shortest man in the crew, and even then, it was cramped.

Cokey "Flo" was a somewhat peripatetic bird, starting out with 861st BS, 493rd BG, moving to 18th BS, 34th BG, in June, then 7th BS, and then back to 18th BS, until finally finding a home with 894th BS, 491st BG. On March 4, 1945, it overshot the runway at BAD 2, and that spelled the end of 44-40486.

B-24J 42-50499 was one of the limited number of B-24s that carried different names on its left and right sides. On the left it had *Open Post* and on the right *Cookie*. It flew with the 458th's 752nd and 755th BSs from July 20, 1944, through to the end of bombing by the group on April 25, 1945. It was transferred to 491st BG for its flight back to the US and ended its days at Altus.

It would appear that 453rd BG was experiencing a delay in the take-off time, as it looks very much like these aircraft are lined up, shut down, on the taxiway. One crew with parachute harnesses on is taking the opportunity to have a crew photo taken. The aircraft is 42-95171 *Diana-Mite*, which collided with another 734th BS B-24 (41-29259 *"Little Mike"*) near Stuttgart on July 21, 1944. Both aircraft exploded. Six of the nine crew on '259 were killed, but the Missing Aircrew Report (MACR) 7253 relating to '171 is missing.

The crew of 42-51594 must have been stretching their fuel to the limit because the report on this 66th BS, 44th BG, says that it crash-landed at Shipdham (the 44th's home base) on February 15, 1945, out of fuel. There is some evidence to corroborate this, as only one blade on one propeller has any damage, so the engines must have shut down within gliding distance of the airfield. 42-51594 was repaired and flew home to storage at Altus.

CB-24D 42-40939 *Donna Mia* looks very smart in a fresh coat of paint. Built originally as a "straight" B-24D, it was modified for anti-submarine patrolling with the Olmstead "Droop Snoot" nose and nose turret. It operated with 479th AS Group until the US Navy rolled the AAF and took AS duties for itself. 42-40939 went to VIII Bomber Command, which sent it to VIII Service Command, which took the turrets out and converted it to a transport. It was used by Special Duties 482nd BG for a short time, and even 458th BG had it in 1945. Its last duty was to check airfield Radio Ranges. Its final fate is unknown as the Individual Aircraft Record Card ends with its departure from the US in 1943, so it is assumed that it ended its days in the UK at one of the air depots.

The Consolidated A-6 hydraulic tail turret as fitted to the B-24D. The turret was progressively improved with larger clear areas for later models, reworked as a nose turret, and eventually it was replaced in the nose altogether by the Emerson electric turret, even by Consolidated itself, as it provided faster tracking speeds.

While the aircraft in the background is 41-29142 *Dinky Duck* of 706th BS, 446th BG, the real reason for having this picture is to show the "metal monster" in the foreground. This is the US Army's maid of all work, like the farmer's tractor, but in "go anywhere" mode with tracks rather than wheels. This is a Cletrac M2 High Speed tractor, which *was* originally built as a farming tractor, but the Army bought lots of them, mostly for towing aircraft on primitive airfields, but as you can see it had other uses too. *Dinky Duck* was salvaged in the UK in June 1945.

453rd BG pilots and navigators receive a briefing before flying a mission. The pilot on the right is wearing a flying Jacket with *Dolly's Sister* on the back. *Dolly's Sister* was B-24H 41-29005, which slipped across the Swedish border into internment on November 21, 1944, after an engine was shot out over Hamburg. It was repaired, repatriated to the UK, and then the US to be stored at Altus in October 1945. It is not possible to be certain what is being pointed at on the map, but it appears to be deep into Germany.

On June 21, 1944, 42-95089 *Dual Sack* of 714th BS, 448th BG, joined the group's attack on Marienfelde, a suburb of Berlin. Over the target, *Dual Sack* was damaged by flak and, unable to make the 4-plus hours return to the UK, headed for Sweden. On landing at Bulltofta, the aircraft ran off the end of the runway into an embankment and crushed the nose. The aircraft and all crew were interned. Twelve other aircraft from this mission also arrived in Sweden.

B-24H 41-28772 did not have a good start. On arrival from the US, it ran off the runway at Connel, Strathclyde. After repair, it operated as a Pathfinder with 482nd BG before transferring in June to 66th BS, 44th BG, where it was named *El Capitan*. It left the 44th for 491st BG (Pathfinders were much in need) in August. A move to 578th BS, 392nd BG, followed, which is where it picked up the large "772" on the nose. The photo was taken on March 10, 1945, on the Bielfeld mission. In the image, it appears to be carrying a replacement vertical tail from a 3rd Bomb Division B-24. It returned to the US postwar and went into storage at Altus.

Dry Run, 41-29137 of 706th BS, 446th BG, was delivered to the AAF at Fort Worth on August 24, 1943. Almost exactly one year later, on August 4, 1944, it was shot down at Bussin (Feurs) in occupied France. By the look of the tracks made by the Cletrac, '137 has just been pushed back into its parking place.

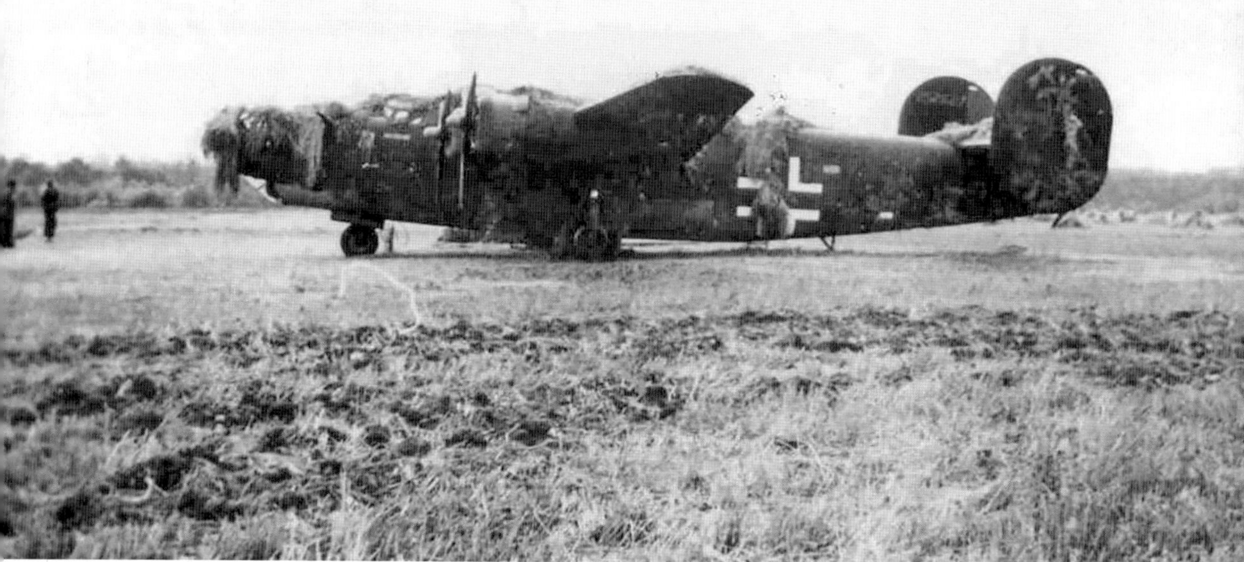

Originally named *Stolen Moments*, 42-52627 of 735th BS, 453rd BG, force landed at Beccles with combat damage on April 29, 1944. It was repaired and sent to 733rd BS and was renamed *Evlibsbunny*. Not so lucky the second time, '627 force-landed on July 12, 1944, at Ensisheim, occupied eastern France (Alsace). It was repaired by the Germans, given German markings and was being prepared for take-off when it was shot up by a P-38 and destroyed, its position having been communicated to the Allied forces by the French resistance organization.

Evlibsbunny burning after the strafing pass by the P-38.

Not a pretty sight and one lost tail gunner. This was what the tail-end of 42-7510 *El Lobo* – 579th BS, 392nd BG – looked like after a very unlucky incident in flight. On December 20, 1943, during the mission to Bremen, it was rammed by the No. 4 engine of 42-7494 *Bums Away* (from 704th BS, 446th BG), which received a direct hit by a burst of flak, knocking the engine off the wing. This happened after 42-7494 tacked on to 392nd BG's formation when the mission was abandoned by the main force due to weather. The engine's propeller slashed through the right rudder and severed the tail turret of 42-7510. A very amateurish "doctoring" of the print was published during the war and has been published since.

Not just *Merchant* as you might initially think, but *Feather Merchant* (slang for a lazy person), 42-94759, one of the original cadre of 4th BS, 34th BG, flew only three missions before being transferred to 862nd BS, 493rd BG. However, when that group re-equipped with the B-17, '759 went into storage until March 1945, when a use was found for it in Italy, joining the 2641st Special Group (Provisional), which became 859th BS. It went to Gioia Air Depot in May 1945 for salvage.

As you can see, it could get a mite crowded in the waist of an 8th AF B-24 with just three people. By the time everybody was rugged up in electrically heated suits, flak vests and flak helmets there was not a lot of room for the gunners to move about without stepping on that aerial photographer crouched over the camera/entry hatch in the floor, especially when, even in a bomber, the floor is not always the floor when in combat!

Leaving no doubt of just what a bomber crew was wishing for, *Final Approach* waits for the next mission all wrapped up against the weather. Every B-24 that left the factory came with a set of operating and maintenance instructions in a leather suitcase and a full set of canvas covers for engines and canopies. 42-52457 lasted exactly a year in combat, from its first mission with 752nd BS, 458th BG, on March 9, 1944, until it was shot down over Lechfeld by flak on March 9, 1944, on its 113th mission.

It is difficult to find fresh unpublished images of a formation ship... and, in this case, I could not! Starting out with 93rd BG's 329th and 330th BSs as *Bucket of Bolts* (suggesting that it had more than its fair share of problems), B-24D 42-40127 was transferred as war weary to 754th BS, 458th BG, where it became the group's first assembly ship as *First Sergeant* on February 2, 1944, flying between March 6 and May 27, 1944. It was salvaged after being damaged beyond repair by fire caused by accidental discharge of flares on the flight deck on the latter date at Horsham St. Faith. It was replaced by a similarly painted B-24H.

A very appropriately named *Flak-Shy* was late model B-24J 44-48903 of 853rd BS, 491st BG. It force-landed on the Continent on February 25, 1945, and was later ferried to BAD 3 for a full repair. It returned to North Pickenham and the 853rd to receive new coding, as its original "Y" code had been given to a replacement. Another repair was necessary when it went off the runway at North Pickenham on April 18, 1945, while taking off on a mission to Passau. The nose wheel tire burst as the aircraft came to a stop near the up-wind end. This was quickly mended, and it returned to the US to end its days in the sun at Walnut Ridge, Arkansas.

There is not much doubt that the artwork on B-24M 44-50529 *Flamin' Mamie* was predominately bright red. Flying just ten missions with 732nd BS, 453rd BG, before being removed from combat and transferred to 852nd BS, 491st BG, its final unit was 406th BS (Night Leaflet), both this and the former were for special duties. Back in the US postwar, its artwork was cut from the fuselage during the salvage at Walnut Ridge, and it is now displayed with the Commemorative Air Force (previously the Confederate Air Force).

Originally intended to be built for the USAAF as YB-24 40-696, the AAF contract was transferred to Britain, and it became LB-30A AM258. The AAF serial was transferred to one of an early batch of B-24Ds. It is seen here at San Diego at a late construction period. Not suitable for combat, it was used on the Return Ferry Service, which returned ferry crews to the US after bringing new aircraft to the UK. It crashed at Prestwick, Scotland, in September 1943.

The burning wreckage of *Lazy Lou* 42-7609 lies at Carlton Scoop after colliding with C-109 42-51766 shortly after take-off from Barkston Heath on December 18, 1944. Originally in combat with 706th BS, 446th BG, it was badly damaged by flak on the June 26, 1944, mission to Bemberg. Removed from combat after repair, it was being used for the training of non-B-24 pilots posted in to fly the C-109s.

A formation of 389th BG B-24s about to cross the English coast on their way to a target in Germany in 1944. The nearest aircraft is 44-40245 *Skerby* of 567th BS, which was shot down by flak on March 24, 1945, over Wesel.

My Bunnie B-24H 41-29567, assembled at Consolidated's Fort Worth factory from Ford parts, began its combat career with 4th BS, 34th BG, and carried the artwork and name *Bambi* on both sides. When the 34th began re-equipping with the B-17 in October 1944, *Bambi* was transferred to 458th BG and assigned to 752nd BS. The left side artwork was overpainted and new *My Bunnie* artwork added; evidence of the painted out previous name is visible. On December 31, 1944, it force-landed on the Continent but was repaired and returned to the unit on March 2, 1945. It met its final fate at Altus. *Bambi* can be seen on p.37.

The iconic image of the air war over Germany in World War Two – contrails galore from a mixed formation of B-24s and B-17s as they head for a target at high altitude.

Foxy Phoebe was serial 41-29527, a B-24H-15-CF of 837th BS, 487th BG. It is photographed here at its home base of Lavenham on May 12, 1944, being attended to by personnel from 1SAD after comparatively minor battle damage. It later suffered a nosewheel collapse on July 2, 1944. As the 487th was one of the groups that "traded in" its B-24s for B-17s, '527 transferred to 576th BS, 392nd BG, where it is known to have suffered relatively severe flak damage to the wing aft of engine No. 2 on January 4, 1945, luckily missing the main spar. Repaired again, it returned to the US on May 30, 1945.

Granted, this is not the best quality image, but there have been a number of mentions of bomb fuses and bomb fusing associated with other photos, so I thought even a grainy but rare image of the inside of the fuse hut of 453rd BG at Old Buckenham was worth including.

This image is from a wartime or early postwar German private photograph, so the quality is relatively low but it is a real one-off. Stripped-out wrecks like this littered Europe for years after the war. *Gashouse Gus* 41-29476 (576th BS, 392nd BG) was one of two 567th BS B-24s forced by battle damage to land on the Continent, in this case Belgium, on March 24, 1945; the pilot appears to have made a very creditable forced landing and the crew were picked up by Allied troops.

A German instructor demonstrates the defensive arcs of fire available to the various gunners of a B-24 to young fighter pilots.

Firefighters at Old Buckenham cover the burning 41-28645 *The Golden Gaboon* from 733rd BS, 453rd BG, in foam on May 30, 1944, after it crash-landed, severely damaged by flak, on return from the Oldenburg mission. Because it blocked the main runway, following aircraft were forced to use the shorter cross-runway, which was affected by a strong crosswind. *Zeus*, a 735th BS B-24 with only the right landing gear down and receiving power from only two engines after being forced to leave the formation and fly home at low altitude and reduced speed, was unable to handle the crosswind, the left wing tip dragged when the aircraft slowed down, and the No. 1 propeller dug into the ground off the runway, causing the aircraft to swing around viciously.

Like the departure queues at a modern civilian airport, B-24s of 754th BS, 458th BG, sit on the taxiway waiting their turn to enter the runway and take off. The last and nearest aircraft is 42-100366 *"Mizpah,"* which later became the group's third assembly ship.

The original ferry crew of 787th BS, 466th BG, had their official squadron photo taken at what appears to be a rather wet and windy Topeka AAB, Kansas, on February 19, 1944, before they left with 42-52598 *Guess who's here?* (with clever artwork) for the UK later that month. After combat damage on May 8, 1944, some wit changed the name to *Guess what's left?* In June, it was transferred to 705th BS, 446th BG, only to be shot down on July 12, over Neuberg by flak.

Bring out the camera and someone has to photo-bomb you. *Hairless Joe* on a photographic session has been joined by a trio of 363rd Fighter Squadron, 357th Fighter Group, P-51s as a series of photos show. 44-40437 was with 861st BS, 493rd BG, at the time, but subsequently transferred to 506th BS, 44th BG, when the 493rd changed to B-17s. 44-40437 was force-landed on the Continent on November 30, 1944, and salvaged in-situ.

"Hard t' Find" (42-50373) is shown here on June 22, 1944, after diverting to Woodbridge because of battle damage the day before. Operating with 839th BS, 487th BG, at the time, it flew missions between May 29 and July 21, 1944, before transferring to 786th BS, 466th BG, to fly more missions until September 11. It was assessed as war weary on September 23, 1944, and salvaged.

All-black B-24s of 492nd BG "resting" at home base Harrington after a busy night's "Special Duties." The date must be post-D-Day because the departing C-47 has D-Day black and white striping visible on the rear fuselage.

Some imaginative artwork on 42-95179 *Here I Go Again* of 752nd BS, 458th BG. 42-95179 flew missions from May 24, 1944, through to January 31, 1945, when battle damage forced it to land near Bridlington (RAF Carnaby) where it was assessed as Category 5 and salvaged.

42-50613 *"Holy Joe"* is seen here before it was relinquished by 391st BS, 34th BG, when the group changed bomb divisions and re-equipped with the B-17. It went into storage until January 1945, when it was assigned to the Mediterranean Theater with 15th AF. There, it joined 764th BS, 461st BG, at Torretto airfield in Italy. When the European war ended, all 15th AF aircraft descended on Gioia airfield for assessment for salvage or return to the US. 42-50613 won the lottery, taking home a crew. The aircraft card is missing, but it would have been placed in one of the huge storage fields until salvaged.

B-24DAS 42-63779 *Hoopoe* is another of 479th AS's aircraft that became surplus when the US Navy took over the role in October 1943. Released to HQ VIIIth Bomber Command by the US-based Anti-Submarine Command, it passed to the VIIIth Service Command (note the badge) where it was converted from a bomber to a transport, a CB-24. Finally moving to 302nd Air Transport Wing of the ATC, it returned to the US redesignated as a C-87 on October 31, 1944. This crew may look cold, but they are probably thanking their lucky stars that they are no longer flying in combat.

Hustlin Hussy – in bright red – was 42-51096 with 734th BS, 453d BG, which was transferred to 704th BS, 446th BG, in April 1945, this date suggesting that this was purely for the purposes of returning the aircraft to the US, since wholesale bombing of Germany stopped on April 25th.

"Briefed at 12:00 Noon and take off was at 3:00 P.M. Our load was 2550 gals. gas, 40-100lb G.P.s. Our target was a railroad junction at the town of Gretz, France" – a waist gunner's diary notes in another 848th BS, 490th BG, B-24 on the mission of June 23, 1944. *Idiot's Delight* 42-94849 did not make its fourth mission for the squadron, as it crashed at Eye on take-off on the above mission, hitting a tree and almost tearing the nose off.

On September 18, 1944, a scratch crew led by Captain Hunter departed from 491st BG's home base of North Pickenham as lead aircraft to drop supplies to 101st Airborne at Veghel, Holland. It was a 34-minute flight at 150ft, climbing to 400ft to drop their supplies. As they turned for home, *I'll Be Seeing You* was hit by flak, the No. 3 engine caught fire, the aircraft went down, slid along the ground, crashed into the haystack seen on the right, and exploded. Nine died, and one survived but was badly burned. 44-40210 was original equipment of 854th BS.

Record photos show the damage caused to B-24J 42-50542 of 853rd BS, 491st BG, when the Metfield bomb dump exploded on July 16, 1944. Soldiers in a hurry to unload dropped one bomb onto another off the delivery truck, and 1,200 tons of bombs and incendiaries exploded, killing six and writing off five B-24s, including '542.

Above and left: Mention has been made on other images of the fact that Ford not only built a large number of B-24s once the factory settled into production, but it also manufactured enough parts for three other factories (Fort Worth, Dallas and Tulsa) to assemble them as well. These parts had to be shipped from Willow Run across the US and these photographs show how it was done – carefully packed in road trailers.

On December 22, 1944, *The Jigs Up* was diverted from Cheddington because of fog and was heading for Valley, Wales, when it ran out of fuel. The crew bailed out, and the aircraft continued on descent and crashed into Mount Holyhead. It was returning from a night mission over Occupied Europe for 36th BS (RCM) at the time. It was B-24J-1-DT 42-51232.

RAF Liberator GR.VI EV882 (AAF serial 42-64289) was initially allocated to 311 Squadron Coastal Command but may never have operated with it, as no operational details can be found. In June, it appeared with 206 Squadron coded 4:L, operating mainly in Norwegian waters from St Eval and Leuchars. In July 1946, it went into storage before being Struck Off Charge in January 1947.

Left and below: Once nose turrets were introduced onto the production line, the B-24 initially carried Consolidated-manufactured hydraulic-powered turrets. Later models used the Emerson electrically powered turret (illustrated), which had a higher traverse speed. In general, the B-24 was a hydraulic aircraft while the B-17 was electric. An interesting fact, not often noted, is that the Emerson had a scale on the top that showed the gunner how many degrees left or right of the aircraft's centerline he was pointing his guns.

A line of new B-24Hs awaiting 8th AF field modifications at BAD 2, Warton, in March 1944. The B-17 to the right (41-9112) is of particular interest, being Maj Robert J. Reed's prototype improved B-17F with nose and tail turrets from the B-24, a number of other armament improvements, less-drag bomb doors, reduced crew numbers and much improved center of gravity. The changes were too much to integrate into the production line without creating extensive production delays, so Maj Reed's "Dreamboat" remained an orphan.

Named *Kentucky Kloudhopper* and flown to the UK by the Vernon G. Alexander crew, B-24J 44-40380 flew four combat missions with 863rd BS, 493rd BG, before being transferred in June 1944 to Special Duties with 851st BS, 490th BG, and subsequently to the RAF 100 Group, as the prototype "Big Ben" project to jam V-2 rockets in the mistaken belief that they were electronically controlled; it was Struck Off Charge with the RAF on December 14, 1945. One wonders if the RAF kept the name.

44-40472 *The Joker* was painted in multicolor and flew with 860th BS, 493rd BG, but on October 12, 1944, moved on to 330th BS, 93rd BG. Surviving the war, it returned to the US at Bradley Field, Connecticut, on May 24, 1945, and by September 24 of that year, had been turned over to the Reconstruction Finance Corporation for storage and salvage at Albuquerque, New Mexico.

As they did on the backs of their leather flying jackets, crewmen often decorated their B4 bags or cases with quite elaborate scenes, but this is one of the best, and black and white really does not do it justice. *King Kong* was 42-50383 of 702nd BS, 445th BG, which flew missions from May 29 until September 27, 1944, when it was shot down on the Rotenburg mission of that date.

'Lil Hoot' was one of the original cadre of 860th BS, 493rd BG. The 493rd, supposedly known as Helton's Hellcats though this is considered to be a postwar appellation, was the last of the heavy bomb groups to be raised for 8th AF, and Colonel Helton had been a Lieutenant in 7th BG LB-30s, which had fought the Japanese war in Java in early 1942. 44-40440 moved to 898th BS, 490th BG, and was written off in a crash-landing on October 31, 1944.

Above and right: B-24H 42-94891 *Mairzy Doats* flew missions with 848th BS, 490th BG, until at least July 27, 1944, when it apparently was transferred out, supposedly to 493rd BG, but just which unit it went to remains unknown, as both units had been flying the B-17 for two months by its loss date, which was October 30, 1944. The complete name was painted on the aircraft before it left the US, but the slab of steel added as flak protection for the copilot covered most of *Mairzy*, and it was never repainted. If you look closely, you will see evidence of the "M" overpainted and part of the "Y."

Fortuitously called *"Lucky,"* B-24D 41-24215 survived the hell of the Ploești oil refinery attack on August 1, 1943, even though it was damaged and made a forced landing in Sicily on the return to North Africa. Repaired, it returned to 93rd BG and, after a few more missions, was declared war weary but flew on as the black and yellow assembly ship with 445th BG, looked after by 703rd BS. Sometimes called *Lucky Gordon*, other photos clearly show just *"Lucky"* painted on.

This will be a familiar sight for anyone who worked in the aviation industry – night maintenance. It is a fairly generic 8th AF World War Two image, bomb group and aircraft identity are unknown, but it is a B-24J-CO, most likely to be in the 44-40XXX serial range, like the aircraft on p.77.

Pappy's Persuader was original equipment of 852nd BS, 491st BG, serial 44-40144. On the other side was a pair of dice. On September 12, 1944, it went down on the group mission to Hanover after flak damage.

44-40879 flew with 714th BS, 448th BG, during July 1944 but was transferred to 652nd BS, 25th (R) BG, to provide photographic, weather and ECM functions (general reconnaissance, basically) for the Army in Continental Europe, where it was named *The Rockaway Babe*. On September 22, 1944, it crash-landed at Warton and collided at high speed with parked 41-28921, shearing off its entire rear fuselage, destroying itself in the process.

RAF Liberator GR.V BZ786 of 311 Squadron of Coastal Command, which operated from RAF Talbenny in Wales; the stub wings are designed to carry rockets. Built as B-24D 42-63810 at Fort Worth, it joined the squadron in September 1943 after Coastal Command modifications in Prestwick, Scotland. In January 1944, it moved to 86 Squadron but quickly went to 1674 Heavy Conversion Squadron as a trainer. In August, it was converted as a transport. It saw further squadron service in this role until it was sold as scrap in March 1947.

Rum Dum, 42-51230, was a Special Operations B-24 with 36th (RCM) Squadron equipped with Mandrel III, Dina, Jackal and Mandrel. On the right side, it was named *Li'l Pudge*. It returned to the US after the war and ended its days at Walnut Ridge.

A mix of 8th and 15th AF B-24s and B-17s parked closely together in one corner of Dubendorf airfield, Switzerland, as the end of the war approached. Most of these aircraft were returned to the UK postwar, but some were salvaged on the spot, too damaged to be worth the effort. One or two even made it back to the US, but most were scrapped in England.

There is conflicting information about the fate of *Terrible Terry's Terror*! It flew missions from April 11 to September 27, 1944, when it crash-landed at Willems, about 12km (7½ miles) east of Lille, France, on the 700th BS, 445th BG's mission to Kassel. That was almost certainly the end of the aircraft, but some reports say it was repaired, returned to the squadron and lost on November 29, 1944. The photo shows a pair of gendarmes engulfed in a sea of locals, mainly children.

A close-up view in flight of *We'll Get By* 42-50679 of 579th BS, 392nd BG. This aircraft also flew missions as part of 577th BS and returned to the US to be put out to pasture at Altus in October 1945.

Stand Bye, 41-28668, a B-24HSH (H2X-equipped Pathfinder) from Douglas at Tulsa, departed Langley, Virginia, bound for 482nd BG at Alconbury under the control of ATC but crash-landed in Iceland on March 17, 1944, at its first refueling stopover on the Atlantic route. As can be deduced from the photo, it went no further.

These two images show B-24D 42-40722 *The Little Gramper* at two different points in its career. Originally with 566th BS, 389th BG, it was named after the small reptiles the crew saw while on TDY with 9th AF in the North African desert. It flew over 50 missions before being retired from combat, after which it became the assembly ship for 491st BG, painted yellow with red spots. In both photographs, it appears that the weather was much the same – cold and wet – and is most likely from the same winter (1943/44), since it had been salvaged in autumn 1944.

B-24J 44-10649 became RAF Liberator GR.VIII KG984 and flew Coastal Command patrols with 224 and 59 squadrons until converted to a transport (C.VIII), which it operated as with 220 Squadron until September, after which it was stored until struck off charge in November 1947.

42-95507 *Lady Doris* was another 36th BS Special Operation aircraft, initially at Cheddington as a trainer for CARPET operators (trainee operators for the AN/APT-2 electronic equipment that jammed morse code transmissions) from 2nd Bomb Division groups. The school closed on January 24, 1945, and '507 moved to operations with 577th BS, 392nd BG, on February 21, as seen here. It was sent to Kingman, Arizona, for salvage in November 1945.

Lady Too, 42-95511 of 748th BS, 466th BG, was landing at Attlebridge on December 24, 1944, and while still on the runway was struck by 44-40208 *The Duchess*, which removed the nose of '511. Luckily, Standing Orders had all crew forward of the pilots in the waist for landing and take-off, or else the nose gunner and navigator would have been killed. The extent of damage to '208 is not known to me.

42-52097 *Lonesome Polecat* only flew a single mission with 713th BS, 448th BG, before transferring to 409th BS, 93rd BG, and then on to 577th BS, 392nd BG, where it was shot down by a fighter on April 9, 1944. Here, the army chaplain gives solace to a crew about to undertake a mission. There were no atheists in a B-24 over Germany in 1944.

Little is known of *Lucky Lass* beyond its AAF serial and unit allocations. 44-40157 operated with 857th BS, 492nd BG, then 329th and 328th BSs, 93rd BG, before returning to the US to rest its bones at Altus.

The two aircraft here are shown in a hangar at BAD 1, Burtonwood, undergoing modification for the *Carpetbagger* role. The unpainted B-24 is *Mag Drop* 42-95131, which was sent to three different Special Operations squadrons, the 850th, the 857th and the 859th, before leaving 8th AF altogether and joining 15th AF's 2641st Special Group (Provisional), to which 859th BS had transferred. On April 25, 1945, it was shot down by a Ju 88 over Austria in what must have been pretty much the Luftwaffe's last gasp.

Yuk-Yuk, 42-94899 of 848th BS, 490th BG, did not have an illustrious combat career, being salvaged on June 7, 1944, after crash-landing on its very first sortie the day before, on the group's mission to Lisieux in the evening of D-Day. This would have been the group's third for the day, but it was recalled or abandoned.

Witchcraft is a very well-known B-24 because of the restored ex-RAF, ex-Indian Air Force B-24 N224J (44-44052) of the Collings Foundation, which has been painted in this scheme since March 2005. This photo, however, is of the original 790th BS, 467th BG, 42-52534, which flew on the group's first mission and its last, racking up a score of 130 missions without a mechanical abort, an 8th AF record.

Shown here in its 453rd BG assembly ship guise, *Wham Bam* was originally a combat B-24D, 41-23738 of 330th BS, 93rd BG. When it was ruled war weary, it was transferred and painted with yellow squares over the Olive Drab. Between April and June 1944, it was often flown by Hollywood actor Jimmy Stewart, including accompanying a mission to Bordeaux. The nose wheel collapsed in France in May 1945, while collecting wine and was salvaged as uneconomical to repair. I wonder how they got the wine back?

***"What's Cookin' Doc?"*, that well known phrase of Bugs Bunny, was a popular aircraft name. This one, B-24J-CO 42-110157, was original equipment of 855th BS, 491st BG, but in June 1944, it was transferred to 786th BS, 466th BG. Despite everything the enemy could throw at it and two landing accidents at Attlebridge, it made it back to the US one year after the transfer and was then flown to Altus in October 1945 to die there.**

Lizzy Belle 42-94884 of 848th BS, 490th BG. The B-24 undercarriage, despite being immensely strong in a straight line, did not handle side loads well. It looks as if '884 has lost directional control on landing (at Eye on June 6, 1944 – D-Day – on the second [recalled] group mission for the day) and folded the right main. It has shed its No. 4 propeller, and a small fire has been extinguished by the base fire crew. It was salvaged the following day.

The nearest aircraft is *Lucky Strike*, 42-109812 of 712th BS, 458th BG, which flew missions from March 6 to December 24, 1944, when it was shot down at St. Vith, Belgium; all nine crew members survived. One less crew for Christmas Day lunch back at base! Directly above and trailing smoke from its No. 2 engine is 41-28667 *Jayhawker*, which was interned in Sweden on April 9, 1944, suggesting that this photo could well have been taken on that day.

The identity of this B-24 is not absolutely confirmed – there is no name visible on the left side. 487th BG had two virtually identical B-24s with serials ending in 61; however, as what can be seen of the fuselage code is an "N," and since 2G-N of 836th BS was 42-52761, then I am confident that this is *Lumbering Lizzy* on May 30, 1944, after the nosewheel would not extend. It was repaired, later transferred to 15th AF where it was assigned to 345th BS, 98th BG, and flew until the end of hostilities in Europe. The aircraft card is missing, so its final fate cannot be confirmed, but it was no doubt salvaged at Gioia.

When this happened, 42-7713 *"The Merry Max"* was basically a brand-new aircraft, having arrived at Seething from the US as original equipment with 715th BS, 448th BG, only the day before. The fact that it made a hash of a landing at East Wretham on November 26, 1943, while on a flight to Warton (BAD 2) for 8th AF field modifications suggests that a green crew had become lost in unfamiliar England. It was repaired and returned to the squadron. Its final fate remains unknown.

Margaret Ann II, 68th BS, 44th BG, 42-40071 is seen here undergoing a double engine change in North Africa while on TDY with 9th AF for the Ploești mission of August 1, 1943. Subsequently transferred in September to 15th AF, which assigned it to the 716th BS, 449th BG, it suffered a taxi accident in early November 1944 and became the 716th's "Doodlebug." 718th BS had a squadron hack (41-23724) named *Doodlebug*. By May 1945, it had been assigned to the Gioia Depot as a war weary for salvage. Still, a long life for a B-24D built in December 1943.

AL507 was one of the early model Liberators operated by the RAF. Designated Liberator II, the type had been ordered by France just before it was occupied by German forces, and so the RAF and USAAF each took parts of the order. As seen here, AL507 has returned to the US for installation of the SCR517/ASV Mk.III radar, after which it flew in a range of squadrons in the UK. It was civil registered to British Overseas Aircraft Corporation in 1946 as G-AHYC but was written off in November 1946 after crash-landing at Ayr, Scotland, when the undercarriage became stuck part way up after take-off from Prestwick for Montreal.

42-50626 *My Gal Sal* has been pushed clear of the taxiways and has already become a "Christmas Tree," donating various parts to other aircraft. All turrets have been removed, probably into storage for possible future use, as will the engines. The aircraft will be stripped of anything reusable, and the hulk trucked off to some corner of the field reserved for such things, usually referred to as "the graveyard". It belonged to 506th BS, 44th BG, and suffered a nose-wheel collapse on landing on August 30, 1944, at Shipdham.

A close-up view of the artwork on 41-28851 *"The Near Sighted Robin"* while at Sovdeborg when interned in Sweden. It flew 36 missions with 7th BS, 34th BG. A report written in November 1944, which speaks of the damage that was required to be repaired before it could be made airworthy again, certainly indicates why it remained in Sweden so long before being able to be returned to the UK. Various specialists from interned crews made up a crew that repaired the repairable interned aircraft by salvaging parts from other aircraft so that postwar they could be flown back to England. In August 1945, '851 arrived at Stillwater, Minnesota, for storage and eventual salvage.

B-24H 41-29250 *Old Butch* began its career in 735th BS, 453rd BG, as original equipment of the squadron. It was flown to Old Buckenham in December 1943 simply as *Butch* but became *Old Butch* as aircraft around it failed to return from missions. Its turn came on the return from the Kassel mission of September 27, 1944. It blazed in its No. 2 engine, then one more engine went out, and the aircraft dropped back trying to make it to Brussels but went down in flames after all ten of the crew bailed out over the front lines. Pilot 2/Lt. Bertrand W. Tardiff was on his 27th mission and does not appear to have flown again in combat.

An unusual angle on *Parson's Chariot*, 42-110162, which arrived in the UK as original equipment of 853rd BS, 491st BG, but was transferred out immediately on arrival to 784th BS, 466th BG. It moved on to 786th BS (same BG) after a period in combat, probably after a major overhaul or combat damage repair required it to be "off-line" at one of the large base air depots. Towards the end of the bombing campaign – April 25, 1945 – it is recorded as salvaged, but no reason is known – it probably was just weary, as many much newer aircraft were available to replace it by then.

Pete, the Pom Inspector is another aircraft whose artwork suffers when seen against the color images that exist. *Pete* was originally a combat B-24D (42-40370) of 506th BS, 44th BG, which flew on the August 1, 1943, Ploești oil refinery mission but aborted and landed at Cyprus. Later, it was damaged in an accident and its return to the UK was delayed, so it went to 565th BS, 389th BG. After 54 missions, it was no longer combat-worthy and it transferred to 789th BS, 467th BG, as an assembly ship, painted black with this artwork. On October 27, 1944, the nosewheel could not be lowered and it crash-landed at Rackheath, where it was salvaged. (POM = Preparation for Overseas Movement.)

A line-up of B-24s that were interned in Portugal during the war and were inducted into the Portuguese Air Force. In the rear is 42-63803, which during its ferry to the 478th AS Group became lost and landed in Portugal to become L-6. From left to right they are 42-40772 *Scheherazade* 564th BS, 389th BG, L1; 42-40783 566th BS, 389th BG (no AAF name) *Nao Faz Mal*, L2; and 42-40801 *Kraut Killer* 328th BS, 93rd BG, L-3. They all suffered various fates, none returned to the AAF, and they were eventually paid for by Portugal.

Apparently named *Witchcraft #II* if you take the photo literally, this is actually *Queenie*, 41-28631 of 735th BS, 453rd BG, very badly damaged on April 20, 1944, when the tail gunner was killed and the whole tail assembly had to be changed. It was last traced to the 453rd on a practice mission on November 11, 1944, by which time it was war weary. It was a participant in the August–September 1945 USAAF aviation exhibition held in the shadow of the Eiffel Tower, with a number of other combat aircraft, fighters and at least one B-17. It was repainted (on the starboard side) as *Witchcraft #II* of 790th BS, 467th BG, for the exhibition but retained its 453rd codes and formation markings.

Rack 'em Back, obviously a ten pin bowling term, was 41-29525 of 838th BS, 487th BG, original equipment of the squadron, but as the 487th re-equipped with the B-17, it went back to 8th AF, which transferred it to 15th AF where it was assigned to 344th BS, 98th BG, in February 1945, where it flew until the end of the bombing, despite having been involved in a mid-air collision with 44-10559. In May 1945, it was sent to the Gioia Air Depot and is assumed to have been salvaged there – the depot had a HUGE salvage area of all types at the end of the war.

If aircraft can be considered to have led interesting lives, B-24D 42-40992 certainly qualifies. On arrival in the UK, it was sent to Benghazi as a Ploești loss-replacement for 44th BG but was "intercepted" by 93rd BG in Libya, which assigned it to 329th BS, where it was named *Tennessee Rambler*. Back in the UK, it was transferred to Special Ops units 801st BG (P), 356th BS, 492nd BG, and then 36th BS of the 492nd. It was repainted black for the roles and at some stage was renamed *The Red Ball Express*. By October 1945, it resided at Altus awaiting scrapping.

A look at the B-24 from a different perspective. Two aircraft from an unknown 8th AF BG are watched by the "ground-pounders" in the Wessel area, as they transit the troops at low level on the way to a drop zone to drop supplies for the army in March 1945, during the initial crossing of the Rhine – a decisive point in the war as the Allied armies entered Germany proper.

It is May 10, 1944, and it is the end of *Rose Marie*'s bombing career, having overrun the runway at Debach and hitting a fuel truck. The serial 44-40207 is clearly painted on the tail of this B-24J-150-CO from 860th BS, 493rd BG. It has no group or squadron markings, so it is possible that it was either about to be delivered or had only recently been delivered to the group. Salvage crews are already dismantling the aircraft for everything useful for the group spares hangar and soon the hulk will be dragged away.

The end of the line. This is Kingman, Arizona – a huge flat, dry location where thousands of mainly B-24 and B-17 bombers that had served their country, and others, "well and faithfully" were sent to die. This and a number of other similar locations sprang up throughout the Continental US run by the Reconstruction Finance Corporation, a US government agency that auctioned surplus war material to return funds to the government. Scrap companies would bid for lots and often established smelters on the spot, turning war machines into aluminum ingots for remanufacture into items that the populace had not seen for years because of wartime exigencies. We see it as a sad end, but in today's mindset of recycling, they were doing a good thing.

Other books you might like:

Historic Military Aircraft
Series, Vol. 20

Historic Military Aircraft
Series, Vol. 17

Historic Military Aircraft
Series, Vol. 16

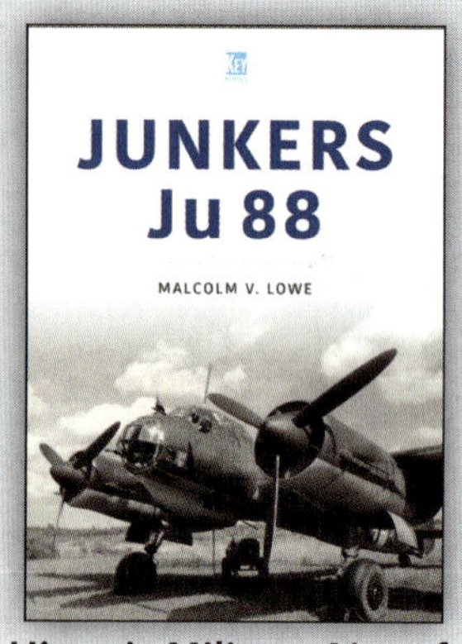

Historic Military Aircraft
Series, Vol. 15

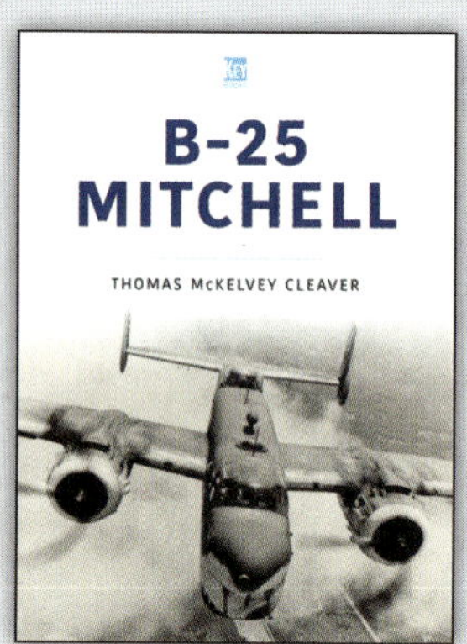

Historic Military Aircraft
Series, Vol. 12

Historic Military
Aircraft Series, Vol. 11

For our full range of titles please visit:
shop.keypublishing.com/books

VIP Book Club

Sign up today and receive
TWO FREE E-BOOKS

Be the first to find out about our forthcoming
book releases and receive exclusive offers.

Register now at **keypublishing.com/vip-book-club**

*Our VIP Book Club is a 100% spam-free zone, and we will never share your email with anyone else.
You can read our full privacy policy at: privacy.keypublishing.com*